BEARS, BEARS, BEARS

by Nora Winter

HOUGHTON MIFFLIN

Boston • Atlanta • Dallas • Geneva, Illinois • Palo Alto • Princeton

There are many kinds of bears. There are brown bears, black bears, and polar bears. This book tells about the food bears eat and the places they live.

Some bears are black and other bears are white. Some bears are small and other bears are very big.

Polar bears live in cold places. Their
fur and fat help them stay warm.

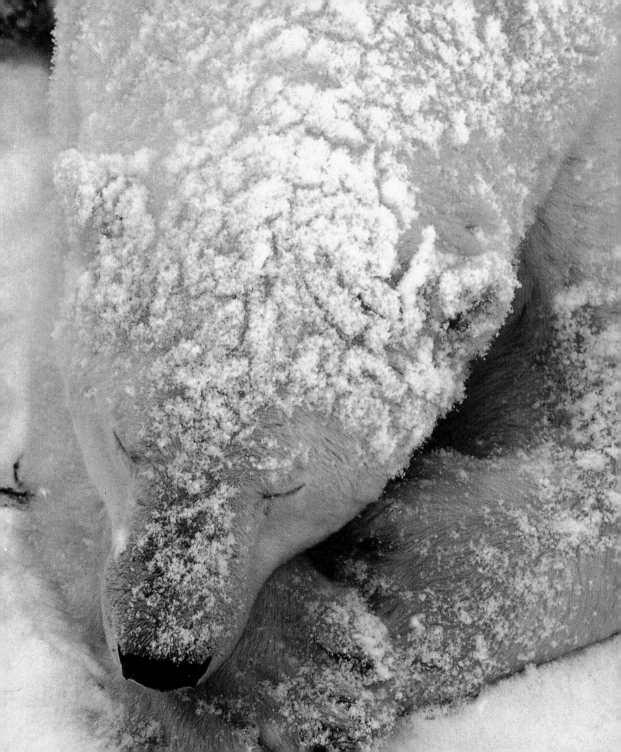

Brown bears like to eat fish.
They wait for fish to swim by so
they can catch them and eat them
for dinner.

The bear sees a fish in the water. It jumps and catches the fish in its mouth. Sometimes the bear eats eight fish for one meal.

Some bears live in the deep, dark woods. They eat wild berries, bugs, and honey. This black bear has sharp claws that help it climb tall trees. There is tasty honey to eat at the top of trees.

Some bears eat nuts, acorns, roots, and leaves. They need to eat a lot of food to get ready for their winter sleep. Bears sleep in the winter because it's cold and there isn't much food to eat.

It is winter now. The polar
bears are getting ready to sleep.

In the winter, some polar bears dig dens in the snow. Some bears find caves or dig holes in the ground. The bears go to sleep for the winter in the dens or in the holes they dig.

Baby bears are born in the winter. They are called bear cubs. Two bear cubs are born at the same time. Sometimes just one cub is born, but there can be as many as four cubs. The small cubs stay close to their mothers.

The bears wake up and leave their dens in the spring. The mother bears teach their cubs how to hunt for food to eat.

Bears can be black, brown, gray, or white. They can be big or small. Some bears live in cold places with snow and ice. Some bears live in the woods. They eat many kinds of food, such as fish, berries, and honey.

Bears don't bother people. But if a person bothers a bear, watch out!

Facts About Bears

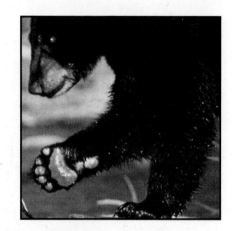

BLACK BEARS

- They can grow up to six feet tall.

- They go into camps to look for food sometimes.

- They can eat eighty pounds of food in one day.

BROWN BEARS

- Some can grow up to nine feet tall.
- They can weigh up to 800 pounds.
- Grizzly bears are one kind of brown bear.

POLAR BEARS

- Their white fur blends in with the snow and the ice. This helps them hide from their enemies.
- They have fur on the bottom of their feet so they won't slip on the ice.
- They are good swimmers and can stay underwater for a long time.